i have
been going
*crazy.*

AF392198

# i have
# been going
# *crazy.*

ABU BAKR ZAFAR

© 2021 Abu Bakr Zafar

All rights reserved to the copyright owner. No part of this publication may be reproduced, distributed, or transmitted in any form or by any means, including photocopying, recording, or other electronic or mechanical methods, without the prior written permission of Author or Auraq Publications, except in the case of brief quotations embodied critical reviews and certain other non-commercial uses permitted by copyright law. Printed in the Islamic Republic of Pakistan.

Printed:       July, 2021            Cover:          Tajwar Rashid
Edition:       1st                  Layout:         Abu Bakr
ISBN:          978-969-749-129-2    Compiled by:    Aspiring Pens
Price:         Rs 1000 PKR, $10 US

www.auraqpublications.com | raabta@auraqpublications.com
@AuraqPublications | @AuraqBooks +92-300-0571-530
Printed and Bound by *Passive Printers* - www.passiveprinters.com

# POEMS & PROSE BY

*Abu Bakr Zafar*

i have been going *crazy*

to

6/9/20 – 09/9/20

i have been going *crazy.*

# PREFACE

I wrote this book when *I was going crazy*. I wrote this for everyone who goes crazy. You understand this phenomenon really well, when so many things are making sense to you yet none of them is true and, sometimes truth is right in front of you while you choose to believe that; it's just in your mind, not the truth and vice versa.

Every day, your life has a different face. Each day turns out to be quite distinct from your expectations. You plan the coming day— everything you think of goes in vain & yet, you don't feel like giving up because you know/think that you just have been going crazy, nothing else.

Sometimes you witness *mergence* and you take a long breath and say "finally" and, yet another day you see it all *colliding* and you're panicking but it ends too.
Next time you see it *merging*, you will fail to be able to believe it. "It's illusion— a trick", you tell yourself. You no longer fall for that for a while but, hey; we are humans, we fail to resist it for long and, the moment you take another long breath and say "finally", *mergence* stays and you wonder, "I was about to settle in *collision*". It's all together now, at one place and then — then it's all colliding again. You're going crazy— again.

i have been going crazy.

While being in the midst of this storm, mergence &
collision make it all a *mess*. A *mess* where nothing
makes sense. It's all here and there, as you believe it's
finally getting all together again, it starts falling apart
and when you say, you are okay with *collision* now,
*mergence* makes it way again.

It's all *mess*, my friend. I know it happens. Everybody
goes crazy. *I have been going crazy* too, when you have
a hard time deciding which way to go or which way is
the destiny and what you have to believe in. what is
the truth actually?

In the midst of that storm, while being a mess, you
make scenarios. You have been looking for answers of
why all of this is happening and there is no answer so,
you give yourself answers. You *overthink,* you go far
away from what is truth. But, what is truth?

By the end, after you adapt all the mergence &
collision and you decide not to choose one because it
goes both ways. You adapt even the mess and the
overthinking that comes with it. It's natural but only
the one going through it can understand the intensity
of insanity.

Overthinking so far, in a human experience is one of
the most toxic, helpless & hurtful condition. One that
turns around the whole meaning of who we are and
how we have been. It takes immense amount of panic

i have been going crazy

attacks, mental and emotional breakdowns to adapt overthinking.

The ending part, where we are okay with everything, where things aren't normal like the way they were anymore but, you aren't moving. You are okay with everything. That, my friend, is *patience.*
A calm after storm and I don't want to say it but, this calm may look like the end of the war but it can be more dangerous to a human than the storm that passed.

People might start liking you for not being violent & emotionally broken anymore rather for acting more sensible and stable, but deep down you're prisoned and living the way that is twice as hard for you but you have got no other option. It's equally good and equally a sign of "something is about to happen"

# AUTHOR ABOUT WRITING THIS BOOK

This book is the poetic journey of a human being, going crazy in love. One of the most powerful reason for someone to go crazy is being in intense love. This book is the description of everything a human can possible feel and think of, in the different phases of his insanity in love. The different phases that has been described in the book are mergence, collision, mess, overthinking and then patience.

Going crazy (that is a phrase I used for someone experiencing all of the above phases in sequence, is obviously an irregular phase of life that isn't static and where things doesn't make sense).

Everything written in this book are the
*overwhelming thoughts,*
*intense feelings,*
*overthinking and*
*chaotic scenarios*
 one makes up in his mind
while going crazy.

But it always ends with a sunrise, always patience has its way to hug us and even though we aren't okay, we act okay. We have to, because going crazy for so long can kill us.

i have been going *crazy*

i have been going *crazy*

*For every single person who goes crazy*
*or have been going crazy, including myself.*

i have been going *crazy.*

# mergence

/ˈmɜːdʒəns/

to combine, blend, or unite gradually
so as to blur the differences.
it brings joy & ease in life.



*Abu Bakr Zafar*

**FIFTY-TWO SECONDS**

After a week of rain
from the pockets of our eyes,
no wonder she cried more than me,
I didn't ache the less.

it was a rainy night, cold & sad.
I stayed out for a week, no call from
home
sad, but I didn't call either.

at that night I told her
I am coming home even if it's mess
there
I was afraid, she'd say no
she took a long breath and said;
you took so long to decide.

I am waiting for you and tonight—
I won't stop watching the clock.

I gathered my mess and walked,
I swear I wasn't too far
It was a walk of fifty-two seconds.

she knew it's fifty-two
she gave me eighty-two


[2]

*Abu Bakr Zafar*

in those seconds, with my feet
walking
I partitioned my brain into two

one for remembering how my life was,
with her arms around me at home.
*peace was in bulk around us.*

other for the flashbacks
of how the week has been with tears
and ashes of cigarettes all over me.

it took me fifty-two seconds
to frighten my soul with the darkness,
her absence threw me in.

it took me fifty-two seconds
to decide that; I'm not going away
ever again even if she asks me to.

in the remaining thirty seconds
that she advanced me for my return,
we partitioned it into two.

in one I told her my plan
in the other she told me hers.

we still have time left

[3]

*Abu Bakr Zafar*

an infinity of a billions of seconds like
that.
because we planned to draw the same
line.



*Abu Bakr Zafar*

I give life to words
the same way
you give life to me.



*Abu Bakr Zafar*

if I could
I would kiss
the mole
on your chin,
and leave
your lips
thirsty.

[6]
*Abu Bakr Zafar*

your kiss hits
harder in my lungs
than cigarette's smoke.

[7]

*Abu Bakr Zafar*

even with so many people around me
I find myself alone with you.

[8]

*Abu Bakr Zafar*

my pen is my mace
to glorify the lustre
that I see in your eyes,
when you kiss me.

[9]

*Abu Bakr Zafar*

even if the world
starts valuing me
and everything I do.
I'll still
come back
to you.

*to home.*


Abu Bakr Zafar

**THE HOPE IS YOU**

she is the kind of hope
that comes with the aurora
and doesn't go with nightfall.
she lies in me
all I have to do, is to— breathe
to keep her vivacious
and all she does, is residing in there
to keep me breathing.

*the hope I hold onto is— you*
*and none other.*

[11]

*Abu Bakr Zafar*

## LITTLE INSANITIES

I wish I was that cup, you take tea in
that tastes your lips couple of times a
day.
I wish I was the fever that vex you
quite often.
I wish I was the never ending
darkness in you, to feel safe and loved.
I wish I was nothing else but a wound
on your hand that you grope all the
time.



*Abu Bakr Zafar*

**II**

I don't need a cure
to heal my undiscovered scars.
I don't want you to kiss me
or love me
as everyone does in the bed.
I am truly not looking for
your hands over my skin
or your metaphors.
all I need is— you around,
breathing next to me
telling me that
*"I am all that you got
and I am all that you ever needed"*.



*Abu Bakr Zafar*

**MY LOST WOMAN**

something that I missed
in my family,
everything— that I looked for
in people coming in and out of my life
but never had.

every miniature thing
that could make me a better person.
all of it — I find it
in a woman sitting in the company
of her silence
not knowing what was happening
around her.

that woman is everything
I ever needed.
that lost creature helped me
finding myself.

every single atom of my body
prays for her happiness & comfort.
i love her beyond reasons.

I am grateful for every breath
she takes around me.

[14]

*Abu Bakr Zafar*

it started from her eyes
& trust me I don't remember,
what happened after that
I— got lost in 'em.



*Abu Bakr Zafar*

I hated swimming
i am in love with your *eyes* now.

[16]

*Abu Bakr Zafar*

today, the last piece of my cold heart
has *surrendered* to your warm fingers.

— *everyday story.*



*Abu Bakr Zafar*

even the way she
looks into my eyes, soaked in love,
it turns every pore
of my skin, on.

[18]

*Abu Bakr Zafar*

it's 4am,
tell my eyes
they've to sleep.
they aren't
getting out
of
your pictures
that don't
even move.

[19]

# I'D MAKE A GOOD FATHER

I would be a father someday. I have
been throwing petals under my feet
and someday I am going to hold the
sensitive as petal' hands of my
daughter.

the cartoon I never liked, I would be
loving them with her. I would be
buying and gifting makeup stuffs to
her. stuff that I never knew how to
buy.

I hate leaving my work even for my
illness. I'd be leaving it for her little
cry, for the moment I sense her
changing the sleeping posture.

I'd be smiling in pain for making her
smile. I'd keep a check on her every
night as she gets into teenage, just to
make sure she is okay —
something as a kid I never had.

I'd make sure she has me around her
on one call. I am not the definition of
perfection right now, but I am going
to be like a fictional hero for her so

[20]

*Abu Bakr Zafar*

she won't be chanting "men are trash"
in her generation' platform.

I'd teach her what men really are,
starting from home. she never has to
find happiness, comfort and support
in the world.

I'd make sure, she has it since the day
one at home — something that as a kid
I never had.

I'd be a father someday. I'd be
someone's superhero someday —
something that I never had.
*a superhero.*

and, if I am planning to love my
daughter like this. imagine, how
bigger my plans must be to love her
mother.

someone, *she is going be a part of.*
someone who wouldn't just be my
better half but my actual half too.

[21]

*Abu Bakr Zafar*

## KISS WASN'T GOOD

I used to be messed up
low-key and out of my control
haunted by anger issues,

when I met her.
she used to be the letting go type,
patient, kind and forgiving
everything over her self-respect.

we fell in love just like that,
we accepted each other exactly that
way.

what went wrong,
is that we kissed and—
we kissed
pretty hard,
for too long
until our lips started to taste the same.

with the mix, we didn't expect it
to be turn out like this.

She became what I used to be
I became what she used to be.
and we are a room full of mess
in love and in love too much.

[22]

*Abu Bakr Zafar*

she wore the pain
of thousand stitches
of fake smiles
just to cage the pain of her past.

[23]

*Abu Bakr Zafar*

you're God's most beautiful art
that only I own
that— only my lips
have the right to utter something
about
to admire
that— only my pen
has the ability to describe.



*Abu Bakr Zafar*

## YOU ARE WORTHY

*dedication to moonlight*

to the strongest woman I know—
these scars aren't a waste.

they developed you
into something out of reach,
something beautiful,
something worthy
something vulnerable.

I love you not because
I think you are tired or because
you are weak.

you are worth loving
worth everything.

you carry the strength
that even I can use.
you make the monster in me
falls asleep.

you're the graceful art
i have ever come across
because you never let
your sufferings go wasted

[25]

*Abu Bakr Zafar*

you come out of them
by conquering something
untouchable.

you are everything i ever crawled to
live for.


—   *when things didn't make too much
sense*





*Abu Bakr Zafar*

## LIES & TRUTH

*12 January, 10:30pm*

all those things that I say
when I am angry are lies.

never try to wonder where they come
from
never doubt it's falsity it's —
all wrong,
the things I say in anger.

every time I say; "if I go
I'm not coming back if you let me go".
never believe it.

the truth is, even if you lock yourself
I will spend my entire life
in the struggle of breaking that cage.

that's the whole white truth
about how much I secretly love you
while you're actually aware of it too.

I would make home at the gate
of your house
if you won't let me in.

you're so in me and if —

[27]

*Abu Bakr Zafar*

I wouldn't be able to see your lips
articulating my name,
I'm going to shatter & it's true.

I'm saying it in senses
& while knowing what you're to me.
never doubt the accuracy of it.

Never.



*Abu Bakr Zafar*

you won't believe it
if I tell you,
it's 4:19am
and it's just you
all around me.

[29]

*Abu Bakr Zafar*

when we sleep together,
I just want you to breathe
close to me.
*I breathe your breath.*



*Abu Bakr Zafar*

the way you call *my name*
it's the only way
I want my name to be called.

[31]

*Abu Bakr Zafar*

**IS HEALING EXPENSIVE?**

how does it feel?
to hug,
someone who knows
about the scars over your heart,
who has seen the stains
on your soul.

someone who taught you,
"coming late is better
than not coming"

someone who had the courage
to reach your broken heart
and didn't mind
her fist bleeding.

how does it feel
to hug her,
and to let your heart
listen to another heart
that only beats for you.

it's crazy how the bond
of two different hearts
get to find a reason to heal

a reason that is simply

[32]

*Abu Bakr Zafar*

the beating sound
of each other.

[33]

*Abu Bakr Zafar*

she did not just love me
she marked me.
*I'm useless*
*to everybody else.*



*Abu Bakr Zafar*

the wild in you
is the same
wild in me.
we both make
a *beautiful story.*

[35]

*Abu Bakr Zafar*

# collision

/kəˈlɪʒ(ə)n/

a conflict between two bodies caused
by differences & crashing.
it brings sadness.



*Abu Bakr Zafar*

**WITCH**

over and over again
being through the same pain,
my heart called out;

"why don't you get tired,
of breaking
and loving again
of waiting
and drinking again"

I guess she's a witch
with the face as— if it's
stardust over my shoulder.

I am trapped
and now the pain from her
is the only thing I can use
to feed myself
in the prison of her
unconditional love.



*Abu Bakr Zafar*

you will miss
the heart
*that only beat*
*for you*
and just you.



*Abu Bakr Zafar*

it's 3am
and I am lying,
thinking
of your lies —
that seemed
pretty close
to what
i have been
searching for.



*Abu Bakr Zafar*

i asked for nothing
but a calm
fire place in you,
while I was freezing.

you said
you are cold.

and you burnt me
when I was sweating
already.

[40]

*Abu Bakr Zafar*

your existence
leaves stains
wherever you go.
people question
my stained existence.
*should I— tell them?*

[41]

*Abu Bakr Zafar*

i know about my heart
pretty much.
you tell,
does your' deliver a name
while it beats?
because your name
throbs quite often
through my body.



*Abu Bakr Zafar*

detachment is getting stronger
and you are still
not ready to cut the rope, short.

[43]

*Abu Bakr Zafar*

you told me
you understand even
my silence,
and here I am
addressing to you
in my poems
and you ain't gettin'
a damn word.

[44]

*Abu Bakr Zafar*

you touched my soul
but the sad thing is
you just touched
and then you left it
undiscovered.

[45]

*Abu Bakr Zafar*

when she came into my life
she didn't step in
she became my life.
and when she left —
she didn't walk away
she disappeared.
not even once in blue moon
she came back.

[46]

*Abu Bakr Zafar*

## I LOVE YOU

I loved and I loved
more than I could.
I loved with every ounce
of power that left me in.
I swear I loved you —
and for that
I squeezed it out from
every single vein of my body.
I loved you
before loving myself.
I loved you in times
when I couldn't be there
for myself —
I was there for you.
I loved you much more than
I was able to love you
in the situation we were in.
I loved you like I've never loved
anyone or anything.
I loved you & I tried more than
my best
to be there for you
and to make you feel like home.
and you did feel it,
you did embrace it
and you did live in it, happily.
but, out of the blue

[47]

*Abu Bakr Zafar*

i woke up —
and came to know that
it all wasn't enough,
it all went wasted,
'cause you couldn't feel it
the way I wanted to make you feel.
my heart's broken
beyond repair but I am alive.
i miss you, but I can't say
that I love you
because maybe for you
"love" isn't what "love" is
for me.
but I still love you,
I know, I feel it.
your name can't be removed
from my heart,
even if you no longer see it.



*Abu Bakr Zafar*

you cried about
everything
that you lost
and forgot to embrace
what you had —
until you lost it.

[49]

*Abu Bakr Zafar*

## HARD TO GET

I wasn't difficult as much as you made
me. I was looking for nothing but a
presence that could make me feel like
home.
I was nothing but homeless, looking
for nothing but a warm shelter. I was
in internal conflicts of how I want to
be and how I had been my whole life.
what I lived was a life without the
fragrance of roses and what I wanted
was you.
everything seemed dull to me when I
was under your light.
you were the only flower in the
garden of my life that was filled with
thorns.
imagine how it's like to be living
around thorns and making a pillow
out of it.
you were the only healing I could
possibly think of and you were the
only difficult thing to be etched by my
innocence.



*Abu Bakr Zafar*

she promised to be there
in the war I was fighting for her.
she kept her promise,
she was there —
not by my side,
but in the crowd
watching me bleeding.

[51]

*Abu Bakr Zafar*

you weren't okay with me
but you weren't okay without me
either.



*Abu Bakr Zafar*

oh my lover!
you see even
the stars at night,
but you're blind
to the sun
that is in love
with you.

[53]

*Abu Bakr Zafar*

she admires art
and out of all, there's nothing wrong
but hard
to digest that
her favorite is not me.

[54]

*Abu Bakr Zafar*

you may love
the art of every artist
except me
but in no art—
except mine,
you'll find yourself.

[55]

*Abu Bakr Zafar*

## CONSEQUENCES

one night,
after you threw me out —
I stared at your picture
till the sun came up.

through my red sleepy eyes,
there were tears in love
speaking straight to me
telling me not to do this.

it's a picture that doesn't move
*but it will move your heart*
*out of your chest,*
so don't.

I went to job in pain
the next day
invisibly bleeding,
because I didn't listen.



*Abu Bakr Zafar*

## LOYALTY

if you wanna leave, leave.
but I'd rather rot in hell
than putting my name
next to someone else'.



*Abu Bakr Zafar*

I pray something should happen
to me.
maybe then you'll come
and see that I was right the whole
time.

being away from you
makes me insane.

[58]

*Abu Bakr Zafar*

somewhere
in the dream
that I lived
while being
awake,
you and I
are happy
together.

[59]

*Abu Bakr Zafar*

I learnt to be okay
without her
all the day.
but as night comes,
huh!
the idea of her
being with someone else
swallows me.



Abu Bakr Zafar

I dreamed
to kiss you
in rains.
now my eyes
don't stop
raining.

[61]

*Abu Bakr Zafar*

# THE BEST THAT I KNEW

I will say it again
and again and again
"she is the best thing
ever happened to me"
no matter what happens
I can never deny
the fact that she is
still the best thing —
my existence ever got along with.
even if the worst happens,
my words never lie.



*Abu Bakr Zafar*

I wish I was a superhero
so you could admire
something about me.
I really needed your
appreciation.

[63]

*Abu Bakr Zafar*

should I write you a letter
because my wrist is bleeding.

*make it letters.*



*Abu Bakr Zafar*

the way I have loved her
and failed.
even if I think I can
I won't be able to love again.

[65]

*Abu Bakr Zafar*

**MARCH**

there was a time in my life
I started to get high
walking around the same old streets
but with different feeling
that I named "numb".

I had lost myself already
in the cemetery of struggle & hope.

I was a mess and I saw a girl.
a girl who, out of nowhere
came to my sight.
God mercy!

and then I couldn't resist
going into her sight.

she was a lost messy girl
with no intention of breathing
& higher intentions of doing good
to people and herself.

strange! I said
unique creature, doesn't belong here
I guessed.

I felt like a baby carried to a hospital

[66]

*Abu Bakr Zafar*

as I sat around her.

that feeling of wounds being
healed.
that essence of comfort.
that relief!

she was an appealing
creature of God, to people.
she felt a home, to me.

I mean, I felt controlled
by her 'not giving attention', face.

her laugh was beautiful
as if a baby laughs
when you touch her stomach.

like a new day
she speaks to everyone
rising sun is the perfect reference
for the way she smiled.

she was the simplest example of
one in a million.

she was kind
that even her pains have—
witnessed it.

[67]

*Abu Bakr Zafar*

she didn't struggle to
make them leave.
she settled and
made peace with them.

she was the girl
I will never forget stepping into my
life
and turning around
the whole story of it.

she loved a boy
turned him into a man
made him sober
and gave up on him.

I am the man writing this
high and fine
better than ever
settling with the pains &
having peace with them.

I am hollow, I won't survive.
she is vacant, she won't survive.

[68]

*Abu Bakr Zafar*

I was just a heart attack away
from forgetting
that I ever loved her.

[69]

*Abu Bakr Zafar*

## IT COULD BE BETTER IF —

the first war that I have ever lost in
my life time is against a woman that I
love. this is the kind of defeat that I
accept with all my heart and I don't
feel like a failure.

I have survived for days without food
and without love and without light
but i crawled on this earth — every
sand particle has witness it. I couldn't
survive losing you, I couldn't stand
without you around. I felt disturbing
rhythm of my heartbeats right after
the moment it felt that you are no
longer around. I couldn't remember
the few days that I spent without you.
I don't even remember where I was
when you weren't here.

even every little atom of my body is in
love with you and knows your name.
if I live for two days without light or
warmth, my existence doesn't look for
light or warmth, my atoms start
calling your name.

[70]

*Abu Bakr Zafar*

I won't say that you're beautiful so I
have reasons to love you. you're the
most patient person i have never ever
read about in books, watched in
movies or ever seen in real. i am not
just blessed to have you. I should say;
everything I ever craved for in my life
— God has sent you to me for filling all
the loopholes.

if I could, I would live each coming
day of my life, breathing around your
fragrance. we've been through worst,
but we survived every tough time
together. the times, that can break the
strongest mountains into a million
pieces but we survived those times
together — high and in love.



*Abu Bakr Zafar*

**UNSOLVED**

we were supposed to be together
I was supposed to forget the past
and start a new life with you.
It was — all clear in your eyes.

since the day one till now
your eyes have a convincing story to
tell
even though your tongue
isn't in the favor of your sight.

I knew & saw that coming
exactly what you saw coming.
you opened the door,
so was I, having my shoes on to walk
in.

it was supposed to happen
atoms were supposed to collide
but then merged.

Why didn't they?



*Abu Bakr Zafar*

# mess

/mɛs/

a situation that is very complicated
or difficult to deal with.
it brings anger & hopelessness.



*Abu Bakr Zafar*

there are so many lies,
growing up
I've been told
& it's painful today—
realizing it all.

[74]

*Abu Bakr Zafar*

all the complaints
of you
about the darkness in you
will come to an end.
pay a visit
to the place — my heart
beats in.



*Abu Bakr Zafar*

## ART NEVER LIES

being an artist
my art is the best witness of how I feel
about you,
and how nimbly your love is running
through my veins
instead of blood.
i no longer have to tell you or anyone
else
about it
because no one seems to
perceive it and
understand it because
logically, no one is in my heart
and no one has the eyes
that I have.
I love you and my art has
promised me
to keep witnessing it
and keeping it alive even after
I die.



*Abu Bakr Zafar*

I will write so much pain
like I never have
and your eyes will bleed
as you keep turning
the pages.

[77]

*Abu Bakr Zafar*

the funny thing is,
every little moment
that i ever lived;
smiling and laughing,
i have paid enough for that.



*Abu Bakr Zafar*

when I go to sleep
a part of me gets out of my body
sits on the chair in my room
watches and counts the hours I sleep.

[79]

*Abu Bakr Zafar*

here's the goodbye to everyone
who had been with me
pretending to be one of the closest.

[80]

*Abu Bakr Zafar*

every time I start
to walk toward peace,
you walk away from me
my demons walk toward me and—
I walk toward misery.

[81]

*Abu Bakr Zafar*

justifications are for those
who have concerns with your side of
story too.

[82]

*Abu Bakr Zafar*

crying was the last thing
I didn't do in my life
and when I did,
It wasn't valued either—
along with many other things.

[83]

*Abu Bakr Zafar*

loneliness alone is difficult
it's better to share it with some other
loner.

[84]

*Abu Bakr Zafar*

## GREW UP TOO SOON.

*January 6th, 12:02AM*

I was 11 when I stopped sleeping
in the warm & safe blanket of my
mother.

I had that loveless feeling in me
even with love around
I was feeling safer & more alive
in the dark rough blanket with
loneliness
and scaring sounds of my breath.

I thought growing up
is having no shelter and cold blanket.

growing up felt more like silence to
me,
constant overwhelming feeling of
eaten up by demons but standing still.

it was more like screaming
with no sound
bleeding wounds but
no articulation not even a whisper.

it was more like not enjoying
breakfast

[85]

*Abu Bakr Zafar*

and not being excited for pocket
money.

I had no one to teach me
and I thought growing up is
not having someone to teach you.

my friends were never really friends
they were biting my heart
and I was keeping them in there.

until I realize; growing up is
having your friends bite you
and walk all over you.

I thought of a lot of things
as in growing up was coming naturally
to me…


(unfinished)



*Abu Bakr Zafar*

## DEATH EATER

can I tell you a truth?
my heart aches I mean —
for real.
the pain that happens to human
organs
but worst.
not the metaphorical one
the one they say in movies
or write in books for personifying our
pain,
and of course it's not the one
we say when we lose someone.
I am talking about the real one
that makes your whole body shiver
makes your eyes red
and nose bleed
and for exactly sharing;
the one that runs through your veins
to make every pore
aware of the call of death.
please pay me a visit.
I just want to see your ring
if you're still wearing it or not
before I let this pain
swallow my weak bones.

[87]

*Abu Bakr Zafar*

so I'm not the gem,
the one you said I am
at the start.

[88]

*Abu Bakr Zafar*

ever happened that someone who
once belonged to you, is nowhere
around today.

[89]

*Abu Bakr Zafar*

**LAST HUG**

I wanted to have my last hug
while being sober so—
I could tell my drugs that;
her intake is more effective
than all of you.
but— even my last hugger
didn't come.
Why did I even write about
last hug?



*Abu Bakr Zafar*

they both
needed each other.
they both
didn't accept it.

[91]

*Abu Bakr Zafar*

I was swallowed
by this dark life.
in the struggle of
soon having
the brighter one.


[92]

*Abu Bakr Zafar*

why people have to forget
every good thing we do for them
that brings a smile on their face.

why they prefer to remember us
with the pain we cause,
while we are in the utmost
level of pain.

[93]

*Abu Bakr Zafar*

## AFTER YOU LEFT

and that day
I couldn't hold it anymore,
It was worse than ever.

a night before,
I spent hours
grasping myself
stopping my chest from
exploding.

cried like an eleven year' old
teenage high school nerd
after ranking second
with mature burning tears.

I tried to cut down
some of my flesh
to shift the pain outside.

some of my clothes
were helping tears
some, helping blood
from portion wide open
that I cut.

but it didn't work.
but that day —

[94]

*Abu Bakr Zafar*

I saw every door closed
and the superman
of my mother,

ah! the superman
was in her lap
aching & screaming
of pain.

her clothes were helping
with tears and blood.

I saw the disappointment
and pity on her face
and I saw regret of assuming me
to be a superman
on her face.

she saw the broken
and fragile eagle on her lap
who had the crown
of victories,

but the victories
were never needed
but a home, that eagle
always craved for.

my soul mate doesn't know

[95]

*Abu Bakr Zafar*

that the soul
she is responsible of
has been breathing
under a grave—
holding her hand strongly.

and the moment she let it go,
all that happened after that
has been told already.



*Abu Bakr Zafar*

## MY CRAZY LITTLE HEART

I am in love
with the disorganized order of
books in an antique
bookstore

sound of birds
on the early winter mornings.

the smell of freshly
printed books

texture of faded
red-colored
nail paint

smiles that hide
thousands of stories
longing for a midnight walk
to let it all out

drunk, lost & high
hard workers
explaining their reasons
of not stopping

the idea of rolling myself
into a white velvet sheet

[97]

*Abu Bakr Zafar*

that smells like you

meeting green signals
on every road
toward your house

I love the idea
of sharing my name
with you

I love how strangers
become lovers
and a lot more

I love you
most of all
above everything

but I hate the idea
of lovers
turning into strangers
for reasons
that never make sense.

I hate sleeping with thoughts
of planning to share
my life with you
but fail to watch it happening


[98]

*Abu Bakr Zafar*

I hate to see
people not trying
and people trying—
not passionately.

I hate to see
your thirst for tea
burning your mouth

but most of all
I hate to have seen
your tongue being burnt
and not being able to kiss you
after watching you
so carefully & closely.

[99]

*Abu Bakr Zafar*

I heard that
those who accept their mistake
walk like they're not perfect
and try to be better
are good men.
I heard them say that,
but the way I got treated
didn't tell me
that they ever considered me
a good man.

[100]
*Abu Bakr Zafar*

it's only the matter
of few cold weathers
few mornings without sun
few nights without sleep
and few moments
of your heart stopping —
every day.
and everything
will be fine.

[101]

*Abu Bakr Zafar*

how can I be
the need of someone
who already have—
everything needed.



*Abu Bakr Zafar*

what's the purpose of
having something
after learning to live—
without it.

what's the purpose of
not getting it
when you can't live without it
anymore.

what's the purpose of
getting it in the end
after suffering so much and—
not being able to act normal.

what's the purpose of
the middle part,
where we just crave,
crawl to death and suffer
numbness.

what's the purpose of
all of this.

what's the purpose of
even living
when you've to live
in this tragedy.

[103]

*Abu Bakr Zafar*

what's better than
being in your bed at 2am
with a broken heart reading —
poetry of a poet
with a soul, as tired as yours,
heart as broken as
yours is going to be.

[104]

*Abu Bakr Zafar*

my absence
never paused
anyone's life.

[105]

*Abu Bakr Zafar*

I wonder
my silence is ordinary.
once,
it was worth worrying.



*Abu Bakr Zafar*

I spent some time
with myself.
it was good.
don't know why
you left.



*Abu Bakr Zafar*

all I ever wanted
is someone
to share my loneliness with.
*was it too much*
*to ask for?*



*Abu Bakr Zafar*

if you wanna be happy
detach the person you love
from the trauma
you've a hard time
walking away from.

[109]

*Abu Bakr Zafar*

under the grave
it's just a man
as a bag of
dead desires.



*Abu Bakr Zafar*

people today
are so diluted.
they can't
understand
the purity
of poetry.

[111]

*Abu Bakr Zafar*

# overthinking

/ˌəʊ.vəˈθɪŋk.ɪŋ/

to put too much time into thinking about or analyzing (something) in a way that is more harmful than helpful.
it brings self hatred & torture.



*Abu Bakr Zafar*

you stepped into my life,
made me so panic
that I started disbelieving
the life I had before you.

you gave me countless reasons
to fall in love with you
even when I was promising myself
that I won't fall.

you gave me a life
that I never had,
that I have always been
craving and looking for.

you handled me
you loved me and took care
of every piece of me
out of thousand guys
fallin' for you everyday
I was just one of those
but, the way I fell for you
nobody would be able to do it
in this little life time.

I know you are happy with yourself
I know that's the love you need
so I am taking back
every single piece of myself

[113]

*Abu Bakr Zafar*

that I have drugged to worship you.

maybe in this life
we fall in love with someone
and name every single piece of
ourselves
to them, hoping they will accept it
but maybe my love
isn't enough or maybe
I deserve to live without you
or maybe my life
is meant to be lived without you.

as my best friend
my soul mate, partner
as the love of my life.

maybe I am too ruined for you
maybe you haven't seen
what's inside of my heart for you
maybe that's what my fate is.

maybe you were too good for me
maybe I would be too wrong for you
but maybe my love is so true
that's why its unseen.

i live my entire life
longing for a person like you

[114]

*Abu Bakr Zafar*

but maybe that's how fate works
you get to have that person
in bits and pieces
maybe that's what love is.

maybe I don't deserve you
more than you deserve happiness
maybe that's how wishes work
you just wish and they never get
fulfilled.

I just want you to know
that I wish and pray;
whatever I have felt for you
I would be able to take it back,
but it's factually impossible.

maybe taking back all the feelings
would kill me because
maybe my heart isn't strong enough.

maybe I was able to
make you live this life
a million times better than anyone
else
but maybe you weren't made to see it
or maybe you wanted to breathe
and I was intended to make you live.

[115]

*Abu Bakr Zafar*

so now, I am accepting,
it's not a war,
you have chosen the love you needed
and there's nothing wrong
to know that it's not me.

maybe I was intended to love you
in thousands of ways
as a best friend, soul mate,
as a lover, a baby,
and as a shelter where you could
live the way you want.

but maybe that's all I was able to do
and maybe you weren't
destined to live that way.

maybe I was more concerned
with an ugly coffee shop
where you could open up your heart
and I could make you feel at peace

maybe I am not a modern lover
to text you all the time,
but I even became that.

maybe I am an old fashioned
and my romance lies

[116]

*Abu Bakr Zafar*

in talking about the things we never
let out,
and a hug in the end.

maybe watching stars and street
lights
are my things
that is way far from
candle light dinners and long drives.

maybe I wanted to love you
nighty percent for you
and literally ten percent for myself.

maybe that ten percent was
more than enough for a guy
who never even had one percent.

maybe that nighty percent
was too less for someone
who always had so many people
to give her love.

I think I have to pack up my love
because maybe sometimes
we can't get the things and a life
we crave for.

but how I will pack my love

[117]

*Abu Bakr Zafar*

it's too much,
it's everywhere in me
I don't know from where to start.

maybe some movies aren't movies
but just trailers and, worthy.

so I just hope that you should know
how much there is love
in a heart that has an ugly appearance.



*Abu Bakr Zafar*

# patience

/'peɪʃ(ə)ns/

the capacity to accept or tolerate delay,
problems, or suffering without becoming
annoyed or anxious.
it brings hope & positivity.



*Abu Bakr Zafar*

## THEY NEED HELP

It's beyond our knowledge but it's true that;
all of our lives have been written to be spent
in a certain way. Altered from the other. It's
barely a chance that people share the same
life.
But, in love people just develop the same
living ways of their lives so that they merge.
That's what love is all about.

The other side is that; we try to change our
life but let me tell you one thing from
experience, world becomes a really
uncomfortable place. It becomes really hard
to survive. It's just the person who knows
deep down, how he feels. No one can
indicate it, no one can guess it. It can't be
explained. But feeling of unknown is
terrible.

If life is made to be happy and to laugh,
that's how world will become a comfortable
place for you and you will crave to discover
more. It will be hard for you to stay
depressed. Whenever you feel that way, you
instantly start to do the things to keep you

[120]

*Abu Bakr Zafar*

out of that depressed zone.

But for depressed people and people who suffer through anxiety and panic attacks, that's how it happens, because they try to move out of their depressed and emotional phase and try to be dragged toward happiness and joy. Their life becomes twice as miserable as it has been. They suffer emotional pains all the time. They feel like nobody gives a shit about them. They feel like they aren't the priority of any.

It is being requested that if your life supports you to be happy sometimes, or to even like yourself and your life. Put your arm into the life of emotionally weak people and help them with affection and love. Bring them toward a life where they can love themselves. Do it by loving them and keep reminding them.

[121]

*Abu Bakr Zafar*

## IF YOU LOVE THEM, TELL THEM

There is always a need of constant reminder of how important the presence of someone is in your life. They need it.

Some people have the history of making the bad choices and choosing the wrong paths, not because they were like that or they wanted it. It's because they have been standing alone in all those storms of their lives that took all of their confidence and faith in the goodness residing in their heart. That loneliness sometimes, makes people doubt their self.

Their continuous gestures of doubt aren't concerned with how much you love them, sometimes it is concerned to their own performance. They need a reminder that they are doing well because sometimes they fail to see the good in themselves.

Their imperfections that they didn't have a control on and the mistakes that they made in the past surround them all the time, resisting them to be happy and making



*Abu Bakr Zafar*

them feel miserable about themselves every
minute.

Sometimes people do pretty much but they
fail to see it themselves. They need a
reminder, a gesture of appreciation and
words of love to make them feel that they
aren't what they've been and they are
accepted for what they were that they aren't
now anymore. They are needed, required
and loved for the way their heart feels and
respects others.

Sometimes few good words and expressions
of a true heart help so much. Sometimes
they mean the universe.

Feelings delivered through expressions and
gestures help build a man's lost faith in
him.



*Abu Bakr Zafar*

## DEAR, M.

Dear true companion of my life,
I understand how hard it must be for you, to
look at me every day and watching me not
living the best or even close.

I know you cared so much about the version
of me, who was doing nothing but wasting
his life over things that were nothing.

I have always been the true admirer of your
courage since the day I met you. I have
always loved your ability to care even in the
times when you actually needed it for
yourself.

I understand how hard it must've been for
you, to always care and to be judged wrong.
I can't imagine how much pain you've
always kept inside of you, locked behind a
beautiful smile on your face.

But, thank you for being the most
influential person in my life. Thank you for
all the positive reinforcements and even
punishments, with the wholehearted



*Abu Bakr Zafar*

purpose of helping me doing better. I loved
every polite and harsh word, you ever said
to me when I didn't understand your
ideology about my better life.

Thank you for listening to my stories that
you call rants. I pray a lot for you and for
your life. I just want to let you know that,
everything you ever did for me, was never
wasted. It always worked and I am forever
thankful for your unconditional love and
affection for me.

Life has never been easy for you. Sometimes
it was so brutal to you that you weren't left
with any option other than being immune.

But, I want to let you know in the end that, I
love you and I am never away from you. I
am as close to you as you are to yourself.
You have loved me equally, in my good and
bad times but more in my bad and I am no
different than you when it comes to loving
you back.

Even if a hundred people are there to love
you and to listen to you, I am going to be the



*Abu Bakr Zafar*

last man standing. I will be the person who
is never going to get tired of you, whether
it's 6pm or 6am. Even at 3am, my ears are
listening to you, my heart is opened for you
and my life has the entire door opened for
you and only you.

Your problems are my problems too and so
is everything you live, go through and feel.

*— to the best friend who doesn't need a
title.*



*Abu Bakr Zafar*

## JUST HOLD ON A LITTLE LONGER

I must say, even though it's hard for me to
stick my faith on it but, things never stay
the same. The hard times end, the good
times arrive. Life is never static for anyone.

I am not that self-loving and hopeful
person anymore, that I used to be but I'd tell
myself this; I should be glad that my hard
times have been with me since my
childhood and it makes me hope for having
good times in future when there'll be the
childhood of someone else under me.

What's gone is gone. I might hate to see my
life falling apart every day but I would
never wish to have my life being this when
I'd have kids and a family.

So, deep inside of me, I tell myself that; I
should be glad that I suffer all the pains and
hardships today and tomorrow is going to
be good. Tomorrow in future, when I'll have
a family of my own, my life won't be falling
apart and I am going to be able to make
lives of others, beautiful.

[127]

*Abu Bakr Zafar*

I want to live over this hope with faith that
my test will soon be over and God will bless
me with peace where I, unlike others, will
be able to smile at the little most things
because I will have a history of craving for a
real smile and joy, away from the dark.

I am not saying this to everyone but myself
and anyone who is reading the most painful
chapter of their lives. Our sun will rise and
we will be okay.



*Abu Bakr Zafar*

## WHY NOT MERGE?

Why a bond has to be complicated and sour
enough to swallow. Why two people have to
be away while being together. Why the
problems are always there as a third person
(specifically as an enemy).

Why not, adding little pieces of sweetness
in it to make it easier to swallow. Why not
making a list of all the complications and
make time, sit together and figure a way out
together.
Why not seeing the problems as challenges
and face it together rather than having one
sword alone in your wars against problems.

Why not seeing the problems as a difficult
journey that two people can together travel
to, get bruised and have the help of each
other in first aid.

Why not, holding on to each other so firmly
that the past won't be able to pull any one of
you back? Why not introducing yourself to
the past of each other so that what holds
you back, should know that it won't be

[129]

*Abu Bakr Zafar*

pulling you alone but someone else along
too. And two is more weight to pull than
one.

Why not living in present and be happy
about the little things. Why not laugh at 8 in
the morning and keep discussing it till 8 at
night.

When you're bonded to someone, it is not
necessary to be on same page. Sometimes
you can watch her favorite TV show and
sometimes she can watch your favorite too.
It's a way to merge.

As long as two people are doing it together,
it's never hard; it's never boring, it's never
impossible.



*Abu Bakr Zafar*

## LITTLE MERCY TO YOURSELF

There aren't many kinds of love. There's
just one. Love, that is acceptance, trust,
support, understanding and spirit of
togetherness as one.

So many of the people who are reading this
right now are so good at loving their special
one but they don't have the same feeling
about themselves, that includes me too.
They accept the flaws of someone they are
in love with, but when it comes to accepting
your own-self with flaws, it seems
pathetically impossible.

It seems easy to love someone but equally
difficult to love yourself. Why? Because the
person we love gives us so many reasons to
love them that include their efforts to make
you feel loved as well as their rigidity with
relationships they share with you, despite
of everything, you love them because no
matter what happens they stick with you.
That's a solid reason for loving someone.

But this same, is what we fail to appreciate

[131]

*Abu Bakr Zafar*

in ourselves. Haven't you been standing still
with yourself through every storm? Don't
you wake up every morning with a hope of
good no matter how brutal the night was to
you. You still try, always do, to make your
life better, to fight your demons. You didn't
give up. We say we are done with our lives
but we still carry it on.

Isn't it a huge reason to love yourself for all
that you've been through but still hope for
good? That dim light in you, that slow voice
in you, is you my friend. Someone, who
deserves to be loved by you before being
loved by anyone else. That you in you,
deserve a coffee date with you, that you
deserve a chance to be hugged by you.
Listen carefully and don't be cruel to
yourself.

World loves you, your family, friends and
your partner loves you. That's obvious. But
they can't love the part of you that is
supposed to be loved by you at the first
place. Once you accept the love by yourself,
you'll come out and feel the strength and



*Abu Bakr Zafar*

courage to accept the love that is already
around you, consistently given to you by
your loved ones.

You did the hard part perfectly, my friend
that is; loving others. It's time that you
should do the easier part too.

[133]

# THE GOODBYE

It was a long time, away— somewhere, at a
place I never knew existed. it was a place
where not everybody goes. some don't
choose to go, some don't really need it,
because they are developed in a place like
that, since forever.

a place where only the people with the most
miserable life, struggling to keep their heart
alive, go. they see it as the last hope and
they come back better.

we all do make mistakes, but some of us
accept them as our mistakes. people like
this have a better chance of changing. there
are some who do wrong and never accept it,
in fact they don't even know that they are
doing wrong. they have no life.

a person should always be a trying person.
someone who always tries to stop making
mistakes, who always knows his doings.
that's how you eradicate them.

[134]

*Abu Bakr Zafar*

I have accepted all the wrong doings of
mine and moreover I accept that I have
been wrong at many places but I couldn't
see that, even if people really close to me,
helped me see it.

I say goodbye to my dark past that seemed
so bright to me but it was a mere lie. it was
manipulation of demons. they put ease in
wrongful paths so that people choose it, but
God says; *right path is always hard to walk
on but it's where a man should walk.*

my heart bleeds in tears to apologize to my
loved ones for all the pain I have caused
while being blind. I apologize to myself for
doing wrong to myself, my life, my love, my
future, my mother and my raising.

demons and the tasteful sins always have a
plan of ruining us and this is where we go
blind.

I promised myself to keep the eyes of my
heart open and to always remind myself;
what is right and what isn't and my mind

[135]

*Abu Bakr Zafar*

promised me to always help me in it,
because both have suffered a lot.

life is hard, really hard. pain, everywhere.
but God made the peaceful part in it too, to
live and to make it better.
please be kind, be patient, be helpful and be
humble. it's the hard way but the right way.

goodbye.

xx



*Abu Bakr Zafar*

RIP



*Abu Bakr Zafar*

Printed and Bound by *Passive Printers* - www.passiveprinters.com
Printing press that offers Print on Demand (POD) Facility.
Printed in The Islamic Republic of Pakistan. 

www.ingramcontent.com/pod-product-compliance
Lightning Source LLC
Chambersburg PA
CBHW030324160726
47992CB00005B/2148